CW00433110

taking up
GOLF

 Golf Foundation

with the

 **Professional
Golfers' Association**

Queen Anne Press

QUEEN ANNE PRESS
a division of Lennard Associates Limited
Mackerye End
Harpenden
Herts AL5 5DR

First published in Great Britain in 1994

British Library Cataloguing in Publication
is available

ISBN 1 85291 551 X

Typeset in Berkeley Old Style
Reproduction by Yale Press Ltd
Printed and bound in Spain

Contents

Young people can learn from top players such as Severiano Ballesteros.

Starting Golf

In the past twenty years golf has become one of the most popular sports in the country. Many people have been attracted by the challenge of a game in which there are no umpires or referees, no need for other players to be present to make up a team and which requires no great athletic ability. The challenge of golf lies in controlling a ball with a club over an area of land which has been specially designed to test, in varying degrees, the skill of the player.

The first requirement for anyone who wants to start golf is to have the enthusiasm and motivation to do so. It may be that your interest in golf was sparked by watching one of the big professional tournaments on television or it may be that there is a course near your home and you have tried your hand at caddieing for some of the members or perhaps a member of your family plays. Many schools are involved in the Golf Foundation Coaching Scheme for Schools and Junior Groups so if your school is among them then you can enrol for tuition.

Your first step should be to approach your local golf club and speak to the secretary about the possibility of joining the club. The secretary will inform you of the procedure and you will probably be asked to fill in an application form and go on a waiting list. This system applies at private golf clubs but not at public golf courses where all you have to do is pay a fee every time you want to play.

If you have never played golf before then it is essential that you receive some tuition from a qualified professional teacher who will be a member of the Professional Golfers' Association. Most golf clubs have a PGA Professional attached to the club and you do not have to be a member of that club to go and have some lessons. Alternatively, you may prefer to visit a driving range, many of which also have Professional instructors. At the driving range you can pay to hit balls without having to retrieve them or worry about losing any!

Golf is a difficult game to master, indeed most golfers never really master all its complexities but that does not prevent them from enjoying its challenge every time they play. So do not expect miracles the first time you try to hit a golf ball: put your trust in the Professional who is teaching you and let him or her guide you along the correct lines.

Young people find it easier to learn the game than adults and are more adept at imitating the movements required in a golf swing. If at all possible, visit a

Nick Faldo, left, and his inspiration Jack Nicklaus, above.

The Course

professional tournament when there is one in your area and watch and study the best players' swings. This will give you a clear mental picture of how the golf swing works and help you in your progress. Remember that many of the game's top players started when they were very young. Severiano Ballesteros started out as a boy caddie on the course near his home in Spain and learned to play using just one club. Nick Faldo was attracted to golf by watching Jack Nicklaus on television - he went on to play alongside Nicklaus in the world's major championships.

If your motivation to play golf is strong enough then you will quickly learn to exercise some control over the ball and discover the satisfaction of hitting it in the intended direction. Once this occurs you will be ready to embark on the great adventure that is golf – the game of a lifetime.

The appeal of golf is that it is played in the open air on land which is pleasing to the eye. The land has been designed by a golf course architect to create 18 holes, or in some cases nine holes, of varying lengths which provide a variety of different shots for the player. A full round of golf comprises 18 holes which usually measure between 5,000 and 7,000 yards in total length. There are shorter courses and longer courses, but generally they fall between these two distances.

Golf courses are usually divided into three different types. Inland courses are generally referred to as 'parkland' courses or 'heathland' courses while courses located on the edge of the sea are referred to as 'links' courses. Parkland courses have many trees upon them and these form an integral part of their design; heathland courses generally feature heather, gorse or broom in their layout; links courses have very few trees and are noted for the large sand dunes which dominate the surroundings. When golf first began in Scotland during the 18th Century, play took place on a strip

The home of links golf, St Andrews. Inset right, a tree-lined inland course, Woburn Golf and Country Club.

The Course

of land between the mainland and the sea. This 'link' between the sea and the land was usually common ground and so the golfers of the day played on it, hence the derivation of the term 'golf links'. Gradually grass took hold on this land and play took place between the great sand dunes the sea had piled up over the centuries. These links courses are unique to Great Britain and form an important part of the heritage of the game.

Parkland courses are man-made whereby the golf course architect has surveyed the land and, using the natural topography, has created the 18, or nine, best holes within the confines of the area available.

Golf course architecture is a highly professional occupation requiring great knowledge and creative instinct. The architect has

to view a piece of land covering some 100 acres or more and from it create 18 different holes, each varying in length, that will provide the player of any standard with a suitable challenge. The basic requirements for any full 18 hole course are that it should have four long holes measuring between 476 yards and 550 yards, four short holes measuring between 120 yards and 245 yards and ten medium length holes measuring between 246 yards and 475 yards. The holes should be laid out to create a rhythm to a round, that is to say the long and the short holes are placed to break up the pattern of medium-length holes. The holes should run in varying directions so that the wind will come from

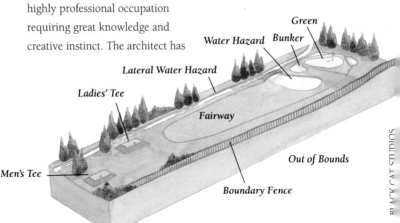

differing aspects and parallel holes should be avoided. Finally the architect makes judicious use of natural hazards such as trees, streams, ditches and ponds while also adding additional hazards such as bunkers so that they create the direction of a path the player ought to take to the hole. In many instances the architect offers the player two routes on the same hole, one difficult and one not so difficult, and it is up to the player to select the one which suits the player's capabilities.

Each hole on the course commences from the 'teeing ground', usually built up above normal ground level, where the ball is placed upon a small wooden or plastic peg called a 'tee peg'. The ball may only be placed on the tee peg on or behind an imaginary line between two markers on the teeing ground and no further behind than two club lengths. Every swing aimed at making contact with the ball is counted as a 'stroke', even if there is no contact with the ball (known as an 'air-shot'). Play is continued from the teeing ground and strokes are counted with various clubs until the 'green' is reached.

Between the tee and the green, the turf is prepared in at least two grades: smooth, short grass known as 'fairway' and longer, thicker grass known as 'rough'. It is interesting to note that the Rules of Golf provide no distinction between fairway and rough, both are known as 'through the green'. Also sited between the tee and the green are the hazards, bunkers or sand traps and water hazards. Special rules apply to both those areas with the main point being that the club may *not* touch the sand or water when addressing the ball. Most courses have boundary fences and once your ball lies outside the boundaries of the course, it is deemed to be 'out of bounds' and that ball is no longer in play.

Once on the green, usually a roughly circular or pear-shaped area of very smooth, fine turf, the ball is stroked along the ground, known as 'putting' and aimed at the hole, $4^{1}/_{4}$ inches in diameter, marked by a flag-stick which should be removed from the hole when putting. Play continues on this basis until the full round of 18 holes has been completed.

Equipment

A full set of golf clubs contains 14 clubs which is the maximum under the rules that can be carried during a round. Sets can be purchased from any golf Professional who will also be able to advise you on the type of clubs that will suit you best.

If you are just beginning the game, it is advisable to purchase a basic set of just five clubs. This number will be perfectly adequate for your initial needs. In many cases, the Professional will have second-hand clubs among his stock and these are worth considering. It is worth remembering that your clubs will last a considerable time and have a re-sale value should you decide to purchase another set later but it is vital to talk to a qualified Professional about your initial purchase.

Golf clubs are divided into two types – woods and irons, referring to the clubhead. As suggested by these names, some are made of wood and some of iron with the shaft usually made of steel or carbon. Nowadays, most woods are made from metal. Each club is numbered although the woods also retain their old names. Thus the number one wood is called a driver, a number two a brassie and a number three wood a spoon. Today's standard set comprises a one, three and five wood. The numbers on all clubs indicate the degree of loft on the clubface. The loft determines the distance and trajectory a golf ball can be hit. A driver has very little loft and is designed to hit the ball, from a tee peg, a long way with a fairly low

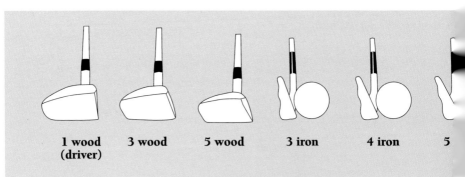

| 1 wood (driver) | 3 wood | 5 wood | 3 iron | 4 iron | 5 |

trajectory. The other woods have greater degrees of loft so the ball will fly higher when struck and not travel as far. It is possible to obtain wooden clubs with even more loft, such as number six, seven or eight, and these are usually preferred by players who find the longer iron clubs harder to use. As a beginner, a three-wood is a suitable wooden club to start with as you can use this club both from the tee and for longer shots from the fairway.

The same numbering system applies to irons which are numbered one to nine plus wedge (W) or pitching wedge (PW). A one iron has hardly any loft at all and is really a club for the very advanced player. Most established golfers start their set of irons with a three iron. The set progresses

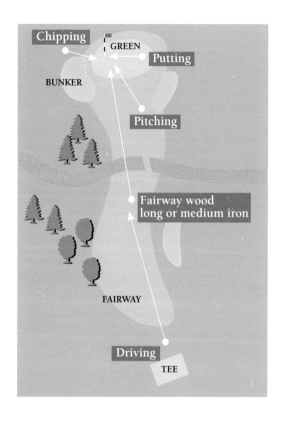

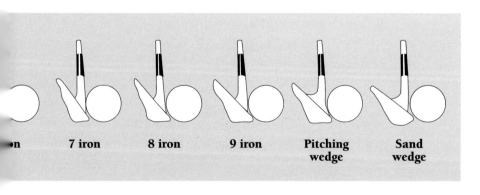

| n | 7 iron | 8 iron | 9 iron | Pitching wedge | Sand wedge |

Equipment

Most Professionals' shops stock a full range of equipment with expert advice at hand.

from three iron to nine iron with each club having a little more loft and the length of the club becoming shorter. After the nine iron come two other clubs called the wedge, or pitching wedge, and sand-wedge. These clubs have extreme degrees of loft and are used for hitting the ball short distances in the air with accuracy. As the name implies, the sand-wedge is specially designed for hitting the ball out of bunkers or sand-traps.

Each club is designed for a specific use, that is to hit the ball a required distance. It is difficult to give the exact distances each club hits the ball because that depends on the player swinging it, but once a player has established the maximum distance with the driver,

then all other clubs should follow in progression.

As far as the new golfer is concerned, one iron club for longer shots, one for medium shots and one for very short lofted, or recovery shots, is all that is required. With these three clubs it takes a short time to learn the distances they will produce in your hands, and, having had professional help at the outset, these three clubs may be added to as your skill develops.

Now we come to the final club in the set – the putter. This is used for rolling the ball along the ground and into the hole. This club has hardly any loft at all. Putters are made in various shapes and sizes and choosing a putter is largely a matter of what looks and feels right for you. Initially it is recommended that you purchase a simple, regular shape that feels under control in your hands and let your fingers be your judge. Weird, fancy shapes may take your eye later on but to start, a basic design will give good enough results. Many golfers fail to realise that between a third and a half of all the strokes made during a round of golf are made with the putter. Therefore, it is important to look for a first-class club with 'feel' and balance as essential qualities.

Golf Bags

You will also need a golf bag to carry your clubs and other items such as golf balls, tee pegs, an umbrella and waterproof clothing. For a basic set of five clubs you will only need a small light-weight bag which can be carried over your shoulder. These bags usually have a ball pocket and a larger pocket for clothing plus an attachment for your umbrella. Golf continues in the rain so an umbrella and a waterproof jacket and trousers can keep you relatively dry during the round.

At this stage, there is no need to purchase a large golf bag of the kind you may have seen being used by the Professionals. Apart from being more expensive than a light-weight bag, they are too heavy to carry on your shoulder and a trolley has to be purchased to wheel them around the course. The other advantage of carrying your bag is that you can walk directly to your ball, whereas with a trolley you have to follow certain routes to keep away from the edges of the greens. A light-weight bag also helps speed up the pace of play.

Golf Shoes

A pair of golf shoes is essential. They must be comfortable, supple, give good foot support and with traditional spikes or composition tread to give your feet a good grip when playing full shots from all sorts of stances on the course. A low cost rubber shoe is very useful for winter golf, but a good investment is a leather pair which ventilates the foot in the summer and a pair of these should be considered as soon as your game begins to develop. Since a player covers over five miles in a round of golf, it is vital to have good-fitting shoes.

One word of warning – never play a full round in brand new shoes – gradually break them in by wearing them for short distances or when you go to the practice ground.

Equipment

Clothing

Fashions for golfers are now
extremely colourful and trousers,
sweaters, shirts and skirts can all
be colour co-ordinated. Sweaters
and shirts should have plenty of
room under and around the arms
for freedom of movement and
should be long enough to cover
the lower back area. Tight clothing
should be avoided at all costs.

DUNLOP SLAZENGER INTERNATIONAL LTD

Golf Glove

A golf glove for the left hand (right
hand for left-handed players) can
help provide a more positive hold
on the club with the usually
weaker hand, thereby giving
constant 'feel' in varying
temperatures. These gloves are
made from thin, supple material to
maximise sensitivity. Many of the
top players, however, remove their
glove for putting to retain the
maximum 'feel' of the putter on
this delicate shot.

The Golf Ball

The ball measures 1.68 inches in
diameter (42.67mm) and weighs
1.62 ounces (45.93gms). The
construction of golf balls is
governed by the ruling bodies of
the game so that one make of ball
does not have any advantage over
another make in terms of its initial
velocity off the club and all golf
balls must not be less than 1.68
inches in diameter nor any heavier
than 1.62 ounces.

*The golf ball has developed over the
years, from the 'featherie' and 'guttie'
through to the dimpled ball as we
know it today.*

16

Golf balls can be manufactured from different components and the three basic types available are as follows:

1. Low compression (softer ball), low cost, one piece composition ball giving reasonable performance.

2. Two piece construction ball of higher performance and including a durable cover.

3. Wound rubber core ball with a durable cover or balata cover for a very high performance. It is advisable to start with the one-piece or two-piece ball as they are less easily damaged and are also cheaper to buy and therefore should cause less concern if they are lost. If you start with a one-piece, low compression ball, as your striking improves you will notice the difference when you move up to a better quality ball.

Etiquette

E tiquette on the golf course is simply good manners. Your first consideration should be for your fellow-players, and it is a case of do as you would be done by.

Do not move or talk when your opponent is about to make a stroke; do not stand too near or on-line with your opponent, always try and stand several feet to the side; never stand too near a player who is practising a swing, golf clubs can inflict nasty wounds; do not shout across the course to a friend, your shout could put off a player on another part of the course. The only time you should shout is to shout the word *'Fore!'* if your ball is likely to hit another player.

Always walk at a reasonably brisk pace, do not loiter as this could hold up the players behind you. Should you lose a ball, always wave the players behind through as this keeps play on the course moving. If you take a divot with your shot always replace it; always repair your ball pitch-marks on the greens and always, without fail, repair your footmarks after you have played from a bunker.

If you are a member of a golf

Etiquette

Always replace divots.

Always repair pitch marks.

Always repair your footprints in a bunker.

club or are hoping to join a club, then you must respect the club rules regarding behaviour and dress. Never tramp through the club in your spiked shoes, they should be put on and taken off in the locker-room. Jeans are unacceptable either on or off the course but casual attire is acceptable in some parts of the club, so make sure you dress accordingly.

Most clubs have starting times for golfers depending on whether two, three or four players are about to play. Please ensure you observe these times.

If you are concerned about golf etiquette, simply watch what established players do and learn by example, but by and large etiquette on the golf course and in the clubhouse is purely a matter of courtesy and common sense.

Basic Rules

A golf course covers a large area of land upon which nature is allowed to progress. Thus a golf course usually abounds with trees, bushes or shrubs and sometimes possesses streams, lakes and ditches.

Ever since the game has been played, golfers have demonstrated a remarkable facility for hitting golf balls into these areas as well as hitting them where they actually want them to go.

In order to cover practically all the contingencies which may arise during a round of golf, a set of rules has evolved which provides the player with a clear guide as to what to do in any particular situation.

There are 34 different rules and they have been framed to make the game as fair as possible. Very few golfers know all 34 rules off by heart but all of them are contained in a small booklet which every golfer should carry on the course. The complete Rules of Golf and Golf Rules in Brief are published by Royal Insurance (UK) Ltd for the Royal & Ancient Golf Club of St Andrews, free of charge, and you should familiarise yourself

Familiarisation with the rules is important for every player.

Handicapping

with the more important rules. The complete Rules of Golf are available from Royal Insurance branch offices and Golf Rules in Brief from the Golf Foundation.

In Great Britain,and many other parts of the world the governing body of the game is the Royal and Ancient Golf Club of St Andrews; in the United States it is the United States Golf Association based at Far Hills, New Jersey. These two bodies work together to unify the rules and deal with all the rules queries because in spite of those 34 rules, instances still occur that are not covered by a specific rule.

The object of the game, as you probably know, is to get the ball into the hole in the least number of strokes. What this number actually totals is dictated by the ability of the player and distance to be covered on each hole.

Each hole on an 18-hole course is given a rating depending on its length. This rating is called 'par' and is the number of strokes an excellent player would need to play a hole without mistakes under ordinary conditions, always allowing two putts on each green. For men, all holes up to 245 yards are rated par three: holes between 246 yards and 475 yards are rated par four: holes 476 yards and over are rated par five. For ladies, all holes up to 200 yards are rated par three; holes between 201 yards and 400 yards are rated par four; holes 401 yards and over are rated

The correct procedure for dropping a ball either for a free drop or under penalty.

Men's tee

Ladies' te

par five. From this you can understand that on par three holes an excellent player will be on the green in one shot, on par four holes on the green in two shots and on par five holes, on the green in three shots.

If you take a standard course of four par three holes, four par five holes and ten par four holes the total par for the course adds up to 72. Some courses that are shorter in total length are rated lower, others that are longer are rated higher.

The par of the course acts as the yardstick by which a player judges performance, and thereby gains a handicap. A very good player would go round in an average of 72 strokes over a period of time. This means that player would have a handicap of zero or 'scratch' as it is called. Some exceptionally good players may go round in an average of two or three stokes under par in which case their handicaps would be plus two or plus three. The majority of players do not reach these exalted heights and their handicaps range from scratch to 28 for men, and scratch to 36 for women.

Thus, an 18 handicap player is one whose average score is 90 on a par 72 course. You can see that it is possible for an 18 handicap player to compete with a scratch player by use of handicap.

No handicaps are applied to Professional golfers.

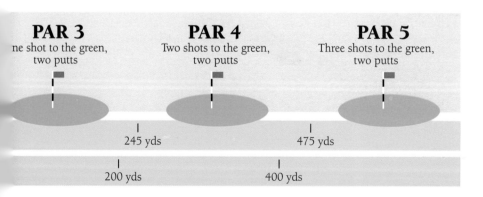

PAR 3
ne shot to the green,
two putts

PAR 4
Two shots to the green,
two putts

PAR 5
Three shots to the green,
two putts

245 yds

475 yds

200 yds

400 yds

Scoring systems

There is only one form of scoring in golf and that is to count the number of strokes made at the ball and that includes attempts to hit the ball that miss altogether!

There are a number of systems to which scoring can be applied.

Stroke-Play (or Medal-Play)

Stroke-play is the scoring system whereby the player counts every stroke made and the player who, at the end of the round, has played the least number of strokes is adjudged the winner. In stroke-play every hole must be completed by the player putting the ball into the hole.

In stroke-play the full handicap is deducted from the gross score and the winner is adjudged on the lowest net score.

Golfers use special terms for their scores on a hole. Finishing the hole with the same score as par is called making par. Scoring one stroke under par is a birdie, two strokes under par is an eagle, three strokes under par an albatross. Scoring one stroke over par is a bogey, two strokes over par is a double-bogey and so on.

Match-Play

Match-play is when players play individually against each other rather than the rest of the field.

In match-play, if player A holes out in five strokes and player B holes out in six strokes then player A wins the hole. The match proceeds in this fashion until one player is more holes ahead than there are holes left to play. Thus, a result which reads that player A

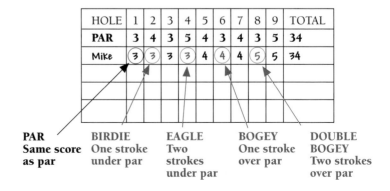

HOLE	1	2	3	4	5	6	7	8	9	TOTAL
PAR	3	4	3	5	4	3	4	3	5	34
Mike	③	③	3	③	4	④	4	⑤	5	34

PAR
Same score as par

BIRDIE
One stroke under par

EAGLE
Two strokes under par

BOGEY
One stroke over par

DOUBLE BOGEY
Two strokes over par

beat player B by three and two means that A was three holes ahead with only two left to play and therefore was unbeatable.

It often happens in match-play that at the end of 18 holes the players are level or, in golfing terminology, 'all square'. If a result has to be achieved then the players return to the first hole and the first player to win a hole is the winner. This is known as 'sudden-death' and from this a result may read that player A beat player B at the 19th or the 21st or even the 24th, depending on the number of extra holes they played before a player won a hole.

In match-play the ball does not have to be holed out as a player may consider that the opponent's ball is so close to the hole that it would be impossible to miss and the putt can be conceded.

Match-Play Handicapping

In match-play a percentage of strokes is given by the lower handicap player to the higher handicap player. For instance, if player A is six handicap and player B is 18-handicap then the difference is 12 strokes, but player

A putt that would be almost impossible to miss may be conceded in match-play.

A is only required to give three-quarters of the difference, so player B would receive nine strokes. This means that on nine holes of the course player B would subtract a stroke from his score before comparing it with A's score. To find out where these strokes are taken, the players look at the scorecard for the column marked 'stroke index.' The stroke index for each hole is adjudged by its degree of difficulty and in this example, every hole with the number '9' or less marked against it would indicate where the strokes are to be taken. This equation is used whatever the difference between the handicaps. If the difference results in a fraction, then this is rounded up or down to the nearest whole

You are allowed to assist your partner in team-play; here Peter Baker and Ian Woosnam study a putt in the 1993 Ryder Cup match.

number. Handicapping means that golfers of all standards can compete against one another each with an equal chance.

Team Play and other Scoring Systems

In golf, two players can play together against two other players as a team, or as a team against a field of other teams. These team competitions usually are played in two different formats:

Foursomes: Foursome golf is played with the partners using one ball between them, driving off alternate tees and thereafter playing alternate shots until the hole is completed. One player drives off the odd-numbered holes while the other drives off the even-numbered.

Below, a typical scorecard showing hole length, par and stroke index.

Markers score	Hole	Yards	Par	Stroke index	Player A	Player B	Ladies yards	Par	Stroke index	Won + Lost - Hlvd 0
	1	462	4	9			425	5	9	
	2	137	3	17			121	3	17	
	3	447	4	3			376	4	1	
	4	479	5	11			421	5	13	
	5	167	3	15			143	3	16	
	6	328	4	13			310	4	11	
	7	362	4	5			333	4	7	
	8	389	4	7			346	4	3	
	9	435	4	1			423	5	5	
	OUT	3206	35				2989	37		
	10	177	3	10			174	3	14	
	11	371	4	6			318	4	4	
	12	468	5	14			448	5	10	
	13	423	4	2			400	5	15	
	14	179	3	18			117	3	18	
	15	458	4	4			405	4	2	
	16	369	4	16			352	4	12	
	17	538	5	8			474	5	6	
	18	486	5	12			458	5	8	
	IN	3469	37				3146	38		
	OUT	3206	35				2898	37		
	TOTAL	6675	72				6044	75		

Competition _____ Date _____
Player A _____ Handicap _____
Player B _____ Handicap _____

Strokes received _____
Standard Scratch Score
72

HANDICAP
NETT

Holes won ____
Holes Lost ____
Result ____

Markers signature _____   Players signature _____

Gauging your progress

Fourball: In a four-ball, each player plays his own ball with the best single score on a hole from one team counting against the best single score on a hole from each of the other teams.

Other forms of scoring include a points system of scoring known as a **Stableford**. This form, invented by Dr. Frank Stableford, awards points for the number of strokes taken at each hole. One point is scored for a hole completed in one over par, two points are awarded for a par and three points awarded for one under par (known as a birdie) and so on.

Players can also play what is known as a **Bogey** competition in which a player competes against the par of the course in match-play form. If a player scores a par then the hole is halved, if the player scores over par then the hole is lost and if the player scores below par the hole is won. The player who is the most ahead of par or the least behind at the end of the round is the winner.

All the forms of scoring used in golf are fully explained in the Rules of Golf.

Golf is a game of progression at which there are no limits on how good a player you can become. When you make your first tentative swings at a ball, even under the watchful eye of a Professional instructor, you may be disappointed with the results. But with practice you will soon experience the satisfaction of seeing the ball fly off into the air in the intended direction.

When you have learned the uses for all the different clubs and different shots they can provide, you will also have an idea how far each club can hit the ball. Obviously a young player will not be able to hit the ball as far as an adult but if you rely on rhythm and timing in your swing you will be surprised how far the ball will travel.

In the initial stages of learning, your golf will be confined to the practice ground where you formulate the basics of the game in conjunction with the Professional. Your first attempt to play a hole on a golf course is a big step but if your preparation has been good and you have learned about etiquette and understand what you have to do, then the challenge is there to be enjoyed.

Whether you have joined a club as a member or are playing on a public course, it is probably sensible to take your first steps onto the course in the company of an established player. If you are a junior whose parents do not play golf, then make enquiries at the club with the Junior Organiser. Most clubs have an adult member with a special interest in young golfers and he or she will be able to help you.

If you are keen and enthusiastic, then, having played one hole on the course, you will probably want to play more. Gradually you can build up the number of holes you play until you feel capable of playing a full round of 18 holes. At this stage you will be fully conversant with the requirements of the game and will also be taking an interest in how many strokes you are taking to play each hole and what your final total is at the end of the round.

This total will give you an idea of what your handicap will be. Although the maximum handicap for men is 28 and for women, 36, many clubs allow juniors who are just starting out to have unofficial handicaps in excess of these figures. Therefore, if the par of the course you are playing is 72 and you go round the full 18 holes in 120 strokes then your junior handicap could be assessed as 48. As we have said before, young golfers improve very rapidly and the more rounds you play, the better your scores become. Once your scores fall into the maximum handicap categories for men and women then you will obtain an official handicap rather than a junior handicap and your scoring will be measured under the official bodies' systems which deal with handicaps for men and women. For men, the system is operated by the Council of National Golf Unions and for women, the Ladies' Golf Union and Irish Ladies' Golf Union. The club at which you play operates these systems on behalf of these Unions.

Many clubs with active junior sections run competitions and you should talk to the Junior Organiser about playing in them. As your game improves, you may be

fortunate enough to win a
competition and this will inspire
you further. If you have an official
handicap, you may also be allowed
to play in competitions against the
adult members of the club and you
will be able to measure your game
against stronger and better players.

There are also opportunities to
play in junior competitions at
other clubs apart from your own
and if you show ability at these
events, then it is likely that you
will be recommended to your
County Junior official as a player

to watch. You could then become
a County Colts player and play
against other juniors from other
counties. A Calendar of Junior
Events is published annually by
the Golf Foundation. If you have
progressed this far then your
handicap will be extremely low,
somewhere in the region of four or
five and you will be able to enter
national championships.

For boys, the major national
championship is the British Boys'
Championship which is open to
boys under the age of 18 on

*A driving range
is a good place
to practise once
you have
mastered the
fundamentals.*

Gauging your progress

Helen Dobson, former British Girls' Champion and Ronan Rafferty, former British Boys' Champion, now both successful professionals.

January 1st of the year of the event and is a very important tournament. The Boys' Championship is a match-play knockout event organised by the Royal & Ancient Golf Club of St Andrews and staged annually at a different course throughout the British Isles. Another important boys' tournament is the Carris Trophy which is held every year and is a four round stroke-play tournament.

For girls, the major national championship is the British Girls' Championship which is open to girls under the age of 18 on January 1st of the year of the event and carries equal prestige to the Boys' Championship. The Girls' Championship is a match-play knockout event organised by the Ladies' Golf Union and staged annually at a different course throughout the British Isles. There are also separate girls' championships for England, Ireland, Scotland and Wales which are also match-play knockout tournaments.

International matches are staged in conjunction with the British Boys' and British Girls'

Championships in which players represent their countries against the other Home Countries.

If you reach these standards then you will probably be playing in the major adult amateur competitions and testing your skills at the highest level. It may be that at this stage you are considering a career in golf as a Professional golfer. This is a momentous step to take and it is advisable to find out all you can about this before making your decision. Information on becoming a Professional golfer is available from the Professional Golfers' Association, whose address is listed on page 64.

The Professional Golfers' Association

The Professional Golfers' Association is responsible for the welfare of some 5,000 professional golfers throughout the UK and abroad. It also promotes the services that its members can provide by way of instruction, advice and the purchase of golf equipment.

Its role includes the provision of a three year training programme for approximately 1,500 trainees who wish to pursue a career as PGA Club Professionals. The Association provides playing opportunities for its members through a National Tournament Schedule and events in each of its seven geographical regions.

There are currently some 5,000 PGA members working in the sport throughout Great Britain and Ireland, and indeed across the world, emphasising the prestige that is placed on membership of the PGA.

Major Championships and Tournaments

There are four championships for men within the world of golf which represent the pinnacles of achievement for a golfer. These are called major championships or 'majors' and are the Open Championship, the United States Masters, the United States Open Championship and the United States Professional Golfers' Association Championship. These events are all held annually on a 72-hole (four rounds) stroke-play basis.

The late Sir Henry Cotton MBE, three times winner of the Open Championship and one of the founders of the Golf Foundation.

The Open Championship

The oldest of the four was first staged in 1860. The Open Championship is always played on a seaside links course in July and attracts entries from all over the world. As an 'Open' Championship it is open to professional golfers and amateur golfers but professional golfers dominate the entry and very few amateur golfers in recent times have come close to winning the title. The last amateur golfer to win the Open, as it is usually called, was the American, Bobby Jones, in 1930.

The Open Championship is staged and organised by the Royal & Ancient Golf Club of St Andrews.

The US Masters

Founded in 1934 by the
aforementioned Bobby Jones, it is
played every April at the Augusta
National Golf Club, the course
which Bobby Jones himself
designed in his home State of
Georgia. The Masters is an
invitational event and entries are
limited to winners of important
professional and amateur titles.
Again, professional golfers have
dominated the list of winners, in
fact, no amateur golfer has ever
won the Masters although one or
two have come close.

The Augusta course is one of
the most beautiful in the world
and the attractions of the course
are conveyed to millions of
households when the Masters is
covered by television.

The US Open Championship

Held in June and staged annually
at a different championship course
in the United States. It is open to
both amateur and professional
golfers and the title is invariably
won by a professional golfer.

The US Open Championship
is organised and staged by the US
Golf Association which is also the

*Above,
Augusta
National Golf
Club, venue for
the Masters.
Left, Greg
Norman
winner of the
Open
Championship
in 1993 with
the trophy.*

The climax of the final hole at the Open Championship at Royal Birkdale in 1991.

body responsible for the administration of the game within North America.

The USPGA Championship

Held in August and staged annually at a different championship course in the United States. Only professional golfers may play in this Championship which is organised by the Professional Golfers' Association of America.

All four major championships receive extensive television/satellite coverage.

Jack Nicklaus has won 18 major championships. Here he rolls in a putt for another birdie on his way to winning the Masters in 1986.

The PGA European Tour

The PGA European Tour is the tournament playing side of the Professional Golfers' Association.

Every year the PGA European Tour administers some 40 professional tournaments. At each tournament, up to 150 professionals compete against each other, usually over 72-holes (four rounds) of stroke-play, for prize-money which is provided by sponsoring companies.

These tournaments run from January to November and are widely covered by the golf magazines, daily newspapers and television.

Similar Tours also operate in America, Australia, South Africa and Japan.

The WPGET

The Women's Professional Golfers' European Tour is a series of tournaments held throughout the year in Europe for women professional golfers. The Tour only started in 1978 but has grown rapidly to accommodate the rising interest in women's professional golf. At each tournament, 100 professionals compete against each other, usually over 54 or 72-holes of stroke-play, for prize-money which is provided by sponsoring companies.

Similar Tours operate in America and Japan.

The World Match-Play Championship

Established in 1964, the World Match-Play Championship is recognised as the most important knockout tournament in men's professional golf. It is held every year in October at Wentworth Golf Club, Surrey over the West course and features a field of 12 of the world's leading professionals.

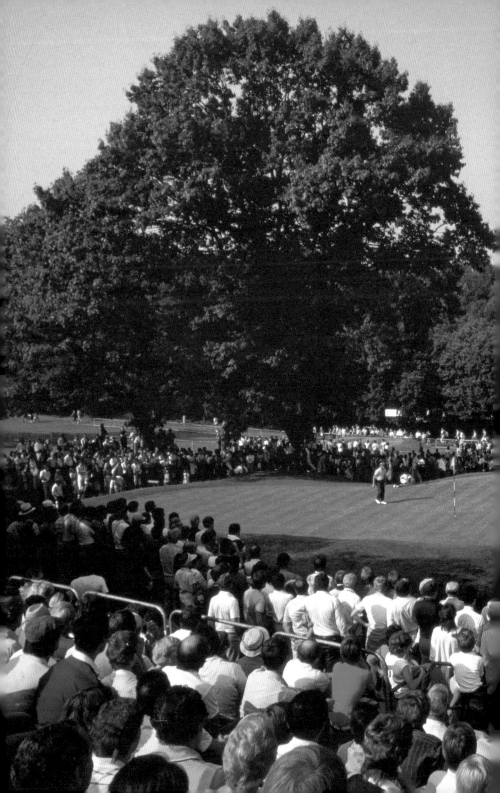

Severiano Ballesteros and Bernhard Langer on the second green at Wentworth in the World Match-Play in 1985. Ballesteros has won the tournament five times, in 1981, 1982, 1984, 1985 and 1991.

Amateur Tournaments

Below, Michael Bonallack OBE, five times British Amateur Champion and now Secretary of the Royal & Ancient Golf Club of St Andrews.

There are a great many amateur tournaments held throughout the year for both men and women. Some of them may only be one day tournaments over 36-holes (two rounds) while others may last almost a week.

The most important of these tournaments are the British Amateur Championship and the British Ladies' Amateur Championship. Both these events are staged on knockout match-play basis and last five or six days. Entry is open to amateurs from all over the world.

The British Amateur Championship is the oldest amateur championship in the world, starting in 1885, and is organised by the Royal & Ancient Golf Club of St Andrews.

The British Ladies' Amateur Championship is also a knockout match-play event. Entry is open to lady amateurs from all over the world. The Championship began in 1893 and is organised by the Ladies' Golf Union. The English Amateur, the Irish Amateur, the Scottish Amateur and the Welsh Amateur Championships are held annually on a match-play basis for male and female nationals of these countries. There are also national stroke play championships in each of the four Home Countries. These tournaments are organised by the Home Union and Ladies' Golf Association of each respective country.

The Home Internationals take place each year when teams from

Mickey Walker, former British Ladies' Amateur Champion and Captain of the 1992 and 1994 European Solheim Cup Teams.

the four Home Countries compete against each other in match-play. There are separate Home Internationals for men and women.

The Ryder Cup

Named after Samuel Ryder, who donated the trophy for the first match in 1927, the Ryder Cup is played every other year between teams of professionals from America and Europe. The match is held alternately on a home and away basis, with 12 players on each side.

The winning 1987 European Ryder Cup Team.

The winning 1989 Great Britain & Ireland Walker Cup Team and the winning 1992 European Solheim Cup Team.

The Walker Cup

Named after George Walker, who donated the trophy in 1922, the Walker Cup is played every other year between teams of amateurs from America and Great Britain & Ireland. The match is held alternately on a home and away basis, with ten players on each side.

The Solheim Cup

Named after Karsten Solheim who donated the trophy in 1990, the Solheim Cup is played every other year between teams of women professionals from America and Europe. The match is held alternately on a home and away basis, with ten players on each side.

The Curtis Cup

Named after Harriot and Margaret Curtis, who donated the trophy in 1932, the Curtis Cup is played every other year between teams of women amateurs from America and Great Britain & Ireland. The match is held alternately on a home and away basis, with eight players on each side.

Basic Swing Techniques

The basics you need to start the game of golf can be considerably simplified by concentrating on three main areas at the outset.

1. How to hold and aim the club.
2. The stance and body position of the address.
3. The swing.

To go beyond these basics in a book of this nature may only complicate and confuse. Our advice throughout is for you to contact a PGA Professional as soon as you possibly can in your golf career. If you have followed the advice we give, a Professional will be able to refine and build a swing to suit your physique and temperament, utilising your natural ability which he or she can see.

Remember that all the following instructions are set out to apply to right-handed players. If you are a left-handed person you need to use left-handed clubs, and of course you must reverse all the instructions accordingly.

Many articles and books start by calling the hold, 'the grip'. It is felt by many leading teachers today that the word 'hold' creates a more accurate description of the type of pressure necessary to provide a firmness, but with the necessary freedom to allow a natural hand action. The word 'grip' suggests tension and extra pressure which is then transmitted to all the other limbs and muscles, hindering a relaxed total action.

1. The hold on the club

The hold must always be taken with the fingers pointing to the ground. This allows the hands and arms to hang naturally from the shoulders. If it is done as most books demonstrate with the palm pointing to the sky the hands will have to be folded onto the handle causing the forearm to be realigned.

The left hand is positioned one inch down the handle with the club positioned across the middle joint of the index finger and half an inch into the palm. The hand is then closed onto the handle. The player should then see two to three knuckles on the back of the left hand and a 'V' shape formed

between the thumb and forefinger should point between the chin and the right shoulder.

Similar to the number of knuckles, the position is flexible due to the size of the player's hands. The left thumb is placed just to the right of centre of the handle as this will support the weight of the club at the top of the backswing.

For the right hand, again with the fingers pointing at the ground, the club is positioned across the middle joint of the index finger passing through the end of the small finger. The hand is then closed onto the handle. The index finger and thumb again form a 'V' that points in the same place as the

one on the left hand. The little finger of the right hand is placed in the gap between the second and third finger on the left hand. This encourages the hands to work together as a unit. A checkpoint is to see if the palms of the hands are facing each other.

The grip pressure should be light enough to make the forearms feel soft. Any tension makes it difficult to achieve a smooth swing.

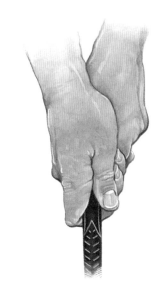

2. The ball position at address

Spreading the feet apart to approximately the width of the shoulders, and keeping both feet almost parallel, the ball position for the tee shot should be opposite a point just inside the left heel. It is easy to check this position by laying a club down on the ground, pointing to the ball at right angles to the target line, and this is recommended as a regular procedure when practising.

For the medium iron shots a slightly more central position of the ball in relation to the stance is used, and for short lofted shots a location of perhaps one inch nearer to the right foot position can be allowed. This encourages the club to strike the ball a more descending blow, creating extra ball control on landing.

Posture The distance you stand from the ball at address depends upon a number of factors, but mainly your own height and arm length. Tilting the upper body over slightly from the waist, the arms should hang naturally and freely from the shoulders which are parallel to the target line. The

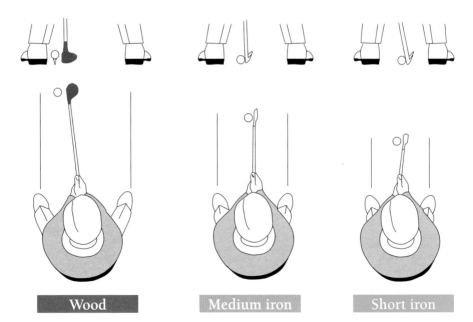

Wood   Medium iron   Short iron

top end of the shaft should be about three inches away from the inside of the left thigh and in line with it.

The knees may be flexed forwards and slightly inwards, but must remain relaxed and without any form of tension.

The chin will be kept clear of the chest to allow the shoulders to rotate freely during the swing. It is essential that the body weight is evenly distributed between both feet with an equal pressure on the balls of each foot.

The procedure for achieving the correct posture.

1   *2*   *3*

3. The Swing

It is essential to have a good 'set-up' as it pre-determines most of the swing movements.

The successful shot requires two elements – Direction and Power.

Direction requires that the blade set square at the set up must be returned to its original position. To this end the club is taken back with the hands and arms, to approximately waist level at which point the wrists will automatically 'set' or cock. This is due to the weight of the club and the

momentum of the swing. At waist level the body weight will have responded and begun to transfer into the right side. Don't resist this movement.

The left shoulder that was introduced into the swing in the takeaway is now turned fully through approx 90°. This is the completed backswing (how high the hands travel is not important). In this position the hips will have resisted the shoulder turn and will have turned approx 45°. This will achieve a feeling of tension around the hips and it is this very tension

4

5

6

7

8

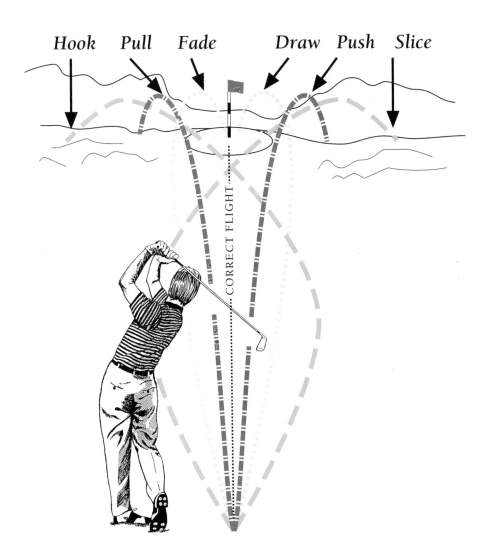

The swing path dictates the flight of the ball.

that is released on the downswing to create the power in the shot. As the tension is released the body weight will now transfer into the left side. The downswing is a reaction to the backswing. At the completion of the follow-through, the hands will finish at roughly head-level and the upper body will point at or to the left of the target. The weight will have completed its transfer and be almost totally on the left side.

This full swing is used on all shots from the driver to the most lofted of clubs. It is the loft that diffuses the power to control the distance.

Most golfers in the early stage of their careers feel a need to hit at a ball. This means the follow-through will be restricted and all power is lost.

The beginner must remember to put in the full follow-through. Swing don't hit!

As the player gets closer to the green shorter more lofted clubs are used to diffuse the power. The ball will fly higher and therefore travel a shorter distance.

When a situation is reached where the shorter club will send the ball too far, the stance will be narrowed and the hands positioned further down the handle. This reduces the length of the backswing. However the player must always be encouraged to follow-through as normal.

How the Golf Foundation can help you

Ryder Cup Captain, Bernard Gallacher provides tuition to young golfers under The Golf Foundation Coaching Scheme.

The Golf Foundation is the National Body responsible for the promotion and development of junior golf.

It was founded in 1952 with the specific aims of introducing more young people to the sport and developing their skills and enjoyment of the game. Throughout its history, the Golf Foundation has steadfastly pursued these aims with the result that thousands of junior golfers have benefited from its work.

The work of the Golf Foundation covers all aspects in the development of a junior golfer and ensures that young people's interest in the game is sustained through to the adult ranks.

The following activities form the basis of the Golf Foundation's work in helping young golfers progress.

The Golf Foundation Coaching Scheme for Schools and Junior Groups

This Scheme forms the basis of the Golf Foundation's work.

Qualified members of the Professional Golfers' Association (PGA) give instruction to students of schools, universities and other places of higher education and to junior members of golf clubs who are in full-time education.

The Golf Foundation pays half the Professional's fee up to a total of 16 one-hour lessons per year for each group. The school/group concerned pays the other half of the costs.

In the case of handicapped children, the Golf Foundation pays the full cost of the tuition.

The Golf Foundation awards vouchers for individual tuition to promising boys and girls.

The Golf Foundation also sponsors Open Coaching Centres during the Easter and Summer holidays and implements a Coaching Award Scheme for Teachers in School who may qualify to organise golf as a school sport and provide elementary instruction to pupils.

The Golf Foundation Eclectic Competition

The Golf Foundation is mindful of the need to sustain competitive interest in the game throughout the school holidays for young players of varying standards.

The Golf Foundation Eclectic Competition fulfils this need by enabling junior members of Golf Clubs to have a target of lowering their score on any one hole each time they play.

Both Scratch and Handicap winners at each Club receive prizes in the form of an inscribed trophy at the conclusion of the holiday period.

The Competition was started in 1978 and each year over 3,000 boy and girl juniors throughout the country are provided with purposeful golf and an opportunity to improve.

The appropriate Master Score sheets and details are available from the Golf Foundation.

THE GOLF FOUNDATION
TEAM CHAMPIONSHIP
FOR SCHOOLS

The Golf Foundation Team Championship for Schools For the R&A Trophy

The Golf Foundation Team Championship for Schools represents a major contribution to junior golf.

The Championship began in 1972 with an entry of 112 teams and since then it has grown to the extent that over 2,000 schools world-wide compete annually.

Throughout its history, the event has helped raise the overall standard of junior golf by providing real competition under championship conditions. Many of the competitors have gone on to achieve international fame at Professional level, including Paul Way, Michael McLean, Peter Baker, Ronan Rafferty, Darren Clarke and Colin Montgomerie.

Teams comprise three players and may be all-male, all-female or mixed. The entries are divided into the four Home Countries and from various qualifying rounds and national finals, the respective winners from England, Ireland, Scotland and Wales go forward to the International Final which also involves schools from Sweden, Germany, France, Holland, Iceland, New Zealand and Australia.

International finalists of the Golf Foundation Team Championship for Schools.

The Golf Foundation Team Championship for Schools is underwritten by the Royal & Ancient Golf Club of St. Andrews which also provides a permanent trophy for the event.

Golf Foundation/Weetabix Age Group Championships

The Golf Foundation/Weetabix Age Group Championships provide competition for boy and girl golfers of 15 years and under in four age group categories. Competitors qualify either through a medal competition at their Club or are nominated by the Club. Regional Finals are then held throughout Great Britain & Ireland during July and August with the Grand Final being held at the end of August.

The Age Group Champion-ships are decided by stroke-play throughout with no handicaps applying and are designed to broaden the scope for young golfers to experience competition in a format that is relevant to their physique and ability.

The Golf Foundation Publications and Visual Aids Service

The Golf Foundation provides publications and visual aids for schools and junior groups.

A number of publications are available which cover the basic introduction to the game. These include guides to teaching golf in school, group coaching, organising a junior section, visual aids to golf technique, a summary of the Rules and Etiquette and a calendar of junior events.

The Golf Foundation also publishes an official magazine 'Tee to Green' which is circulated widely, free of charge, to schools, groups and Golf Clubs throughout the country.

The Golf Foundation

The Golf Foundation Merit Award Scheme

The Golf Foundation Merit Award Scheme is designed to give young golfers of all ages the incentive to improve their skills and technique and also make them more knowledgeable about the Rules and Etiquette.

From the first category (red) to the last (gold), each participant is able to measure his or her progress in a step-by-step manner. At each stage the young golfer's progress is acknowledged by the award of a certificate in the appropriate colour plus, in the latter stages, a bag tag and identity card.

The Merit Award Scheme should be used in tandem with the Golf Foundation Coaching Scheme for Schools and Junior Groups. Professionals and pupils work together to ensure each pupil achieves the maximum potential, while at the same time gaining the maximum enjoyment.

RED

PRELIMINARY AWARD I
Certificate awarded

■ Pupils working with PGA Professionals in the Golf Foundation Coaching Scheme, or any other approved junior coaching scheme, or with school teachers holding a Coaching Award Certificate, should be knowledgeable in the fundamentals of grip (hold), stance, swing and strike.

■ The strike should be performed consistently and the ball should travel reasonably straight. Must be able to hit two balls out of five at least 50 metres for boys and 30 metres for girls, between two markers 20 metres apart.

■ Should have completed at least two lessons.

WHITE

PRELIMINARY AWARD II
Certificate awarded

■ Should have completed at least four lessons in Golf Foundation classes, or in any other approved junior coaching scheme or with school teachers holding a Coaching Award Certificate, including lessons taken during Stage 1.

■ Should be able to complete nine holes and demonstrate a basic knowledge of Etiquette and Rules;

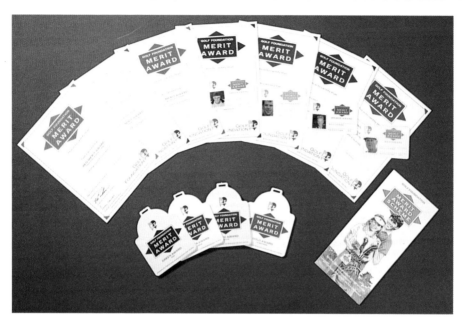

must complete at least two holes in three over par or better and score 24 or better over nine holes on the putting green.

■ The nine holes on the course must be played in the company of one of the following: a PGA Professional or assistant, a Junior Organiser, a Teacher holding a Certificate, or any adult with a recognised handicap under CONGU or LGU/ILGU regulations.

BLUE

PRELIMINARY AWARD III
Certificate awarded

■ Should have completed at least six lessons in Golf Foundation classes, or in any other approved junior coaching scheme, including lessons taken during Stage I and II.

■ Should be able to complete 18 holes under the same conditions as for Stage II and also have a clear knowledge of the essential rules.

■ Should be able to play to 40 over par or better for boys and 54 over par or better for girls.

Certificates, bag tags and identity cards awarded in the Merit Award Scheme.

The Golf Foundation

GREEN

PAR
Certificate, bag tag, and ID card awarded

■ Should have completed at least eight lessons in Golf Foundation classes, or in any other approved junior coaching scheme, including lessons taken in any earlier stages.

■ Obtain at least 50% pass rate on six written questions on the Rules of Golf (from sample sheet Section A).

■ Obtain at least 50% pass rate on six written questions on Etiquette of Golf and Definitions (from sample sheet).

■ Obtain an official handicap of 27 or better for boys and 35 or better for girls.

BRONZE

BIRDIE
Certificate, bag tag, and ID card awarded

■ Must have passed the Green Award.

■ Should have completed at least ten lessons in Golf Foundation classes, or in any other approved junior coaching scheme, including lessons taken in earlier stages.

■ Obtain at least 50% pass rate on ten written questions on the Rules of Golf (from sample sheet Section A).

■ Obtain at least 50% pass rate on ten written questions on Etiquette of Golf and Definitions (from sample sheet).

■ Should have obtained an official handicap of 22 or better for boys and 29 or better for girls.

SILVER

EAGLE
Certificate, bag tag, and ID card awarded

■ Must have passed the Bronze Award.

■ Must be at least two months since passing the Bronze Award.

■ Should have completed at least 12 Golf Foundation group or individual lessons, or any other approved junior coaching scheme, including lessons taken in earlier stages.

■ Obtain at least 75% pass rate on 12 written questions on the Rules of Golf (from sample sheet Section A or B).

■ Obtain at least 75% pass rate on 12 written questions on Etiquette of Golf and Definitions (from sample sheet).

■ Should have obtained an official handicap of 16 or better for boys and 18 or better for girls.

ALBATROSS
Certificate, bag tag, and ID card awarded

■ Must have passed the Silver Award.

■ Must be at least three months since passing the Silver Award.

■ Must achieve at least 80% pass rate on interpretation of ten Rules from the Rules of Golf.

■ Should have obtained an official handicap of nine or better for boys and ten or better for girls.

■ The examinee must produce a sponsor form of approval for the test, countersigned by one of the following: Head or Deputy Head Teacher; County Golf Union Official; Golf Club Committee Member; County Schools' Golf Association Officer; a Professional golfer, other than the regular instructor.

■ The examinee must have played in at least two of the following events: County Junior/ Colts' Championship; County Schools' Championship (team or individual): Golf Foundation Age Group Championships; Regional/ National Schools' Championship; National Junior Championship. (These are minimum requirements; higher levels are naturally accepted.)

■ The examinee must have qualified for two of the following: Won a Boys' or Girls' Section of a

Junior Club event or better; a Junior Open event or better; finished in top three of a County Schools' Championship; reached semi-final of County Schools' Knock-out Championship; finished in top three of a County Junior Championship; qualified at regional level in a National Junior Tournament. (These are minimum requirements; higher levels are naturally accepted.)

With the assistance of a PGA Professional young golfers can progress quickly through the Merit Award Scheme.

Glossary

Ace The ultimate stroke in golf, a hole in one.

Albatross A hole completed in three strokes under par.

Arc The path the club completes through the swing.

Around the green The term used to describe shots played in the vicinity of the green.

 **Ball-marker** This is a flat disc or coin used to mark the position of the ball on the putting green.

Better-ball In which two partners play as a team, the better score of either counting.

Birdie A hole completed in one stroke under par.

Blind (hole or shot) A blind hole is one where the green cannot be seen from the tee. A blind shot is made when a high object prevents the player from seeing the intended flight of the ball.

Bogey A hole completed in one stroke over par. A double-bogey is a hole completed in two strokes over par and so on.

Bunker A hazard filled with sand.

Bye The number of holes left to be played when a match is finished.

Caddie A person who carries the player's clubs.

Casual water A temporary pool of water on the golf course. When the course is waterlogged after heavy rain, the player is permitted to lift and drop his ball clear without penalty if the ball lies in casual water.

Chip A short shot to the green.

Concede A hole is conceded when one player has played so many shots it is impossible for him to win or halve it with his opponent. A player may also concede his opponent's putt if he feels the opponent is certain not to miss. Concessions take place only in match-play.

Dead When the ball lands so near the hole it is all but impossible for the player to miss the putt.

Divot The piece of turf removed when the ball is struck. All divots should be replaced to avoid damage to the course.

Dormie In match-play a player is dormie if he is as many holes ahead as there are left to play, for example, if one player were three holes ahead with three to play he would be dormie three.

Draw The spin imparted to the ball so that it moves gradually from right to left.

Eagle A hole completed in two strokes under par.

Fade The spin imparted to the ball so that it moves gradually from left to right.

Fairway The cut portion of the course between the teeing ground and the green.

Flagstick The pole, usually with a small flag attached, placed in the hole to provide the player with a target. Also called the pin.

Fore! A shout of warning to anyone on the golf course indicating the ball is travelling in their direction.

Four-ball see better-ball.

Foursome A form of golf with two partners per team but instead of playing their own ball as in better-ball, the partners play alternate shots with the same ball and drive at alternate holes.

Free drop Under certain conditions a player is allowed to drop the ball away without penalty. Check the Rules of Golf if in doubt.

Grip The position of the hands on the club and also the top part of the club where the hands are placed, which is usually covered in rubber or leather.

Green Each putting surface on the course.

Greensome A form of foursome in which two players play as a team but each player drives and then the team decides which ball to play in alternate strokes for the remainder of the hole.

Ground under repair Ground which has been repaired by the greenkeeper. The area is usually marked by a small notice.

Halved A hole is halved, or a match is halved when the opponents are level, either in relation to strokes taken at each hole or at the end of a round.

Handicap The figure allotted to every player denoting the average difference between his score and the par of the course.

Hanging lie A downhill lie.

Hazard A bunker, ditch, stream or pond.

Hole The target on the green into which the ball must ultimately fall. The hole is 4$\frac{1}{4}$ inches in diameter. Also the full distance between tee and green.

Holing-out Striking the ball into the hole.

Honour The preference given to the player whose turn it is to drive first. The honour on the first tee can be agreed but thereafter it goes to the player who had the lowest score at the previous hole. If a hole is halved, the player with the honour retains it.

Hook A shot which moves sharply in flight from right to left.

Hosel The point at which the shaft of the club enters the clubhead.

Ladies' tee The teeing ground used by women golfers, usually placed some distance forward from the men's tee.

Lateral water hazard A ditch or stream which, when viewed from the fairway, runs parallel to a hole instead of across it.

Lift and drop under penalty If a ball has to be lifted because it is impossible to play it from where it lies, the player is permitted to lift and drop under the penalty laid down by the rules.

Local rules The rules of golf apply everywhere golf is played but all clubs have additional rules on certain points pertaining to the layout of the course.

Loft The angle at which the clubhead lies in relation to the shaft.

Lost ball Players are allowed to look for five minutes for a lost ball but after that time has elapsed they have to deem the ball lost and play another according to the rules.

Match-play When players play against each other individually or as a team.

Medal-play When the player counts the number of strokes taken during the round. Also called stroke-play.

Obstructions Objects, either movable or immovable, which prevent the playing of a shot.

Out of bounds When the ball is hit over the boundaries of the course or hole, thus incurring a penalty.

Outside agency Any person or animal not involved in the game who obstructs or moves the ball.

Par The rating allocated to a hole or to a course, based on length.

Partner The person with whom one plays either as individuals or as a team.

Penalty When a shot finishes in a lie from which the ball is unplayable, out of bounds or lost, then a penalty is incurred according to the rules. Penalties can also be incurred for infringement of the rules.

Pitch A high, lofted shot played from near the green.

Playing out of turn In match-play, if a golfer plays before it is his turn to play either from the tee or fairway, his opponent may request that the ball be called back and the shot played again.

Playing preferred lies see winter rules.

Pull A shot that flies directly to the left with no hook spin; to hit a shot directly to the left with no hook spin.

Push A shot that flies directly to the right with no slice spin; to hit a shot directly to the right with no slice spin.

Putt The stroke used on the greens and played with a putter.

Round Completing all the holes on the course, usually 18 holes.

Rub of the green Interference with the ball that is put down to fate.

Scorecard The card taken out and filled in by golfers in stroke-play. It has to be filled in by the player's partner, checked and signed by both players.

Slice A shot which moves sharply in flight from left to right.

Standard Scratch Score (SSS) The rating allocated to a course based on length, terrain and degree of difficulty.

Stroke The striking of the ball.

Stroke-play see medal-play.

Tee The wooden or plastic peg on which the ball is placed prior to driving off. Also the teeing ground.

Tee-markers Metal or plastic objects used to mark the forward limits of the teeing ground.

Texas Wedge The term for using a putter from off the green.

Through the green The term used in referring to the whole area of the course except the teeing ground, the putting green and all hazards on the course. The term is also used when a player hits a shot too boldly so that the ball runs over the back of the green.

Trap Also called a bunker.

Winter rules Special rules for play during the months when the course is wet or frost bound. Winter rules allow the ball to be lifted, cleaned and placed within six inches not nearer the hole without penalty, thereby lessening damage to the course. Also called playing preferred lies.

The Golf Foundation

Foundation House
Hanbury Manor
Ware
Hertfordshire SG12 0UH
Telephone 01920 484044
Fax: 01920 484055

The Professional Golfers' Association

Apollo House
The Belfry
Sutton Coldfield
West Midlands B76 9PT
Telephone: 01675 470333
Fax: 01675 470674

Text by
Chris Plumridge

Instruction by
Alasdair Barr, Geoffrey Cotton and John Stirling
Instruction illustrations
courtesy of the PGA

Photography by
Charles Briscoe-Knight, Phil Inglis and Phil Sheldon

Designed by
Vickers Associates